DINOSAURS
THE AGE OF GIANT CREATURES

written by Christina Wilsdon

illustrated by Christopher Srnka

Reader's Digest
Children's Books™

Pleasantville, New York • Montréal, Québec • Bath, United Kingdom

Consultant
Michael K. Brett-Surman, PhD
Museum Specialist for Dinosaurs,
Smithsonian Institution, Washington, D.C.

Reader's Digest Children's Books
Reader's Digest Road, Pleasantville, NY 10570-7000
Copyright © 2001 Reader's Digest Children's Publishing, Inc.
All rights reserved. Text on page 4-5 Copyright © 1999 Weldon Owen, Inc.
Reader's Digest Children's Books is a trademark and
Reader's Digest is a registered trademark
of The Reader's Digest Association, Inc.
Manufactured in China.
Library of Congress Catalog Card Number: 00-104670
10 9 8 7 6 5 4 3 2

Once the dinosaurs were king of the beasts. They roamed Earth for about 165 million years. Today, all that's left of them are fossils—bones, footprints, and other bits. What happened to them? Why did they all disappear about 65 million years ago?

CONTENTS

WHAT WERE THE DINOSAURS?

When you think about dinosaurs, you may imagine huge, ferocious creatures—still frightening even though they have been extinct for millions of years. But not all dinosaurs were large. Not all were scary. In fact, an amazing thing about these animals is how different they were from one another. Some dinosaurs were giants. One of the biggest was as long as three school buses. But the smallest one could fit in the palm of your hand. Most of the meat-eating dinosaurs had sharp teeth and claws to rip their prey apart. But the plant-eaters had smaller teeth with bumps on them to chop up their food. Some dinosaurs had beaks. Some lived by themselves or in pairs. Others lived in herds of a thousand or more.

DO YOU KNOW?

Pterosaurs (flyers) and plesiosaurs (swimmers) were not dinosaurs.

GREAT LIZARDS!

Dinosaur means "fearfully great lizard." But dinosaurs were not lizards. What made them different? They walked like mammals and birds—with their legs straight under them, not sprawled out to the side.

Coelophysis
9 feet (2.7 m) long
This small meat-eater from the Triassic period walked on two legs. *Coelophysis*—which means "hollow form"—had hollow bones.

Despite their differences, though, dinosaurs had many things in common. They all laid eggs, and they walked with their legs directly under their bodies. Most had scaly skin, like a present-day lizards and crocodiles, although some may have had feathers. Dinosaurs can be divided into two groups—those called lizard-hipped and those called bird-hipped, depending on the shape of their hipbones.

Millions of years before our first human ancestors appeared, dinosaurs ruled the Earth. The Age of Dinosaurs lasted 160 million years, during the Mesozoic era. This era is divided into the Triassic, Jurassic, and Cretaceous periods.

Want to know more? Read on and discover what it was like in the days of the dinosaurs!

THAT'S AMAZING

Today we know about more than 800 different types of dinosaurs, and a new type is discovered every seven weeks. Paleontologists think we will eventually find more than 1,000. But there are many dinosaurs that we will never know anything about—they are the dinosaurs that left no fossils behind to tell us about themselves.

LIFE IN THE TRIASSIC

TRIASSIC FACTS
Began 248 million years ago
Lasted 42 million years

One Big World
Triassic life traveled freely across a huge continent called Pangaea, from the Greek for "all Earth." Pangaea included all the world's land.

Imagine that you are on a planet with one giant supercontinent. Warm winds lash the coastlines with rain. Thick forests are filled with ferns and horsetails, while palmlike plants called cycads sprout near the shore. Cone-bearing trees, or conifers, grow inland. No flowers can be seen anywhere and most of the land—away from the sea—is a hot, dry desert.

Welcome to the Triassic period.

Spiders, scorpions, centipedes, millipedes, and insects scuttle among the plants and the desert sands. Reptiles and giant fish hunt other fish in the ocean. More reptiles hunt on land—and these are ancestors of the first dinosaurs.

DO YOU KNOW?

The early dinosaurs shared their world with the first crocodiles, tortoises, and rat-sized mammals.

The First Dinosaurs

Dinosaurs first appeared about 225 million years ago. Some were meat-eaters. Often, they moved around on their two hind legs. They could run quickly and turn easily as they hunted other reptiles, balancing with their long tails as they sprinted. These dinosaurs could use their front legs as well as their toothy jaws to catch their food.

Eoraptor
3 feet (1 m) long
One of the earliest dinosaurs was *Eoraptor*. This small dinosaur ate reptiles the size of lizards. *Eoraptor* fossils were first discovered in South America.

Herrerasaurus
10 feet (3 m) long
Another early dinosaur was also found in South America. *Herrerasaurus* ran on two legs, like *Eoraptor*, but was much bigger. This fierce hunter had three sharp claws on each front foot. It used these claws to hang onto large reptiles even if they struggled hard to get away.

Early Plant-eaters

Not all early dinosaurs were meat-eaters. Some ate plants. These creatures were the first long-necked dinosaurs. Paleontologists have found their fossils all over the world. The first plant-eating dinosaurs had thick, strong limbs. They could stand on their hind legs, but could also walk on all fours. Their long necks let them sweep their heads across the ground in search of food. Many scientists think that these plant-eaters lived in herds because they have often found their fossils clustered together in large groups.

At the end of the Triassic, many kinds of animals disappeared. The early dinosaurs, however, survived—and thrived. They gave rise to new kinds of dinosaurs and spread from one end of Earth to the other.

Plateosaurus
26 feet (8 m) long
Plateosaurus was one of the biggest early plant-eaters. It lived in forested areas in lands that are now part of Europe. *Plateosaurus* ripped apart leaves with its strong, notched teeth. A big hooked claw on each thumb helped it defend itself from predators.

JURASSIC FACTS
Began 206 million years ago
Lasted 62 million years

AGE OF THE JURASSIC GIANTS

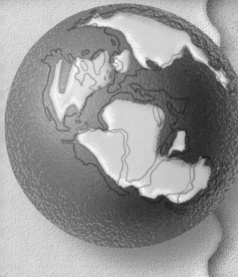

Breaking Up
Pangaea started to split apart. By the end of the period called the Jurassic, there were two supercontinents, Laurasia in the north and Gondwana in the south.

The dry weather of the Triassic and early Jurassic gave way to wet weather. The deserts shrank while the thick forests of conifers, ferns, and cycads spread.

Some of the biggest animals ever to walk on land appeared during the Jurassic. The biggest of these beasts were plant eaters called sauropods.

Sauropods had thick feet and legs rather like an elephant's. They had long necks, so they could browse in the treetops or sweep their heads from side to side to graze on ground plants. Their peglike teeth ripped off leaves, which were then crushed in an organ called the gizzard. An enormous stomach digested the food.

Their huge size helped the sauropods. They were so big they scared off most predators. Some sauropods probably fought off enemies by cracking their whiplike tails at them. They may also have traveled in herds.

Diplodocus
100 feet (30 m) long
Diplodocus was one of the longest dinosaurs at about half the width of a football field.

The Cutting Edge

Jurassic meat-eaters grew bigger, too. One of the biggest ones was *Allosaurus*. It weighed about four tons (4 t) and was about the length of three cars. It stood as tall as an elephant.

Scientists have found sauropod bones with scrapes made by *Allosaurus* teeth. That's how we know that certain meat-eaters hunted live animals that big. In fact, allosaurs may have hunted in packs, like wolves, when they tackled really big prey.

But not all the meat-eaters were so big. Some, like *Ornitholestes*, were about the size of a human and probably hunted small mammals, reptiles, and insects. This kind of food may also have fed a new animal that came on the scene in the late Jurassic—the first birds.

Stegosaurus
20 feet (6 m) long
Sauropods weren't the only Jurassic plant-eaters. Stegosaurs had bony back plates that may have helped them warm up or cool down. These slow-moving animals used their long tail spikes for defense.

Brachiosaurus
82 feet (25 m) long
Brachiosaurus was one of the heaviest sauropods. It weighed up to 50 tons (50.1 t)—about as much as 10 bull elephants! Its front legs were much longer than its hind legs, and its head reached as high as a five-story building.

Allosaurus

40 feet (12 meters) long

Allosaurus strode on strong hind legs. Each of its front legs had three fingers with claws measuring 6 inches (15 cm) long. Its massive jaws were lined with curved, jagged-edged teeth up to 4 inches (10 cm) long that easily slashed through such prey as this young *Brachiosaurus*.

DO YOU KNOW?

Allosaurus did not chew its food. It didn't need to—it could gulp its food in huge chunks!

THE AMAZING CRETACEOUS

CRETACEOUS FACTS
Began 144 million years ago
Lasted 79 million years

Over a long period of time, Jurassic dinosaurs such as *Allosaurus* and the stegosaurs slowly disappeared. So did most of the sauropods. Other groups of dinosaurs took their place in the Cretaceous period.

One of these groups was the tyrannosaurids. This word means "tyrant reptiles." The star of this group, *Tyrannosaurus rex*, ruled the North American continent in the Late Cretaceous. This meat-eater was one monster appetite on two powerful legs. Its terrifying jaws flashed sixty sharp teeth as big as bananas.

Worlds Apart

The continents continued to break up. Laurasia spread across the ocean to form continents in the north, and Gondwana split into the southern continents and many islands. One sea divided North America in two. Different kinds of dinosaurs grew in the west and the east.

The Cretaceous started out warm. But by the time it ended, temperatures dropped. The North and South Poles became colder places.

Armored Tanks

Ankylosaurs like the *Pinacosaurus* (11.5 feet/3.5 m) grew thick skin protected by bony slabs and sharp head spines. Heavy bone formed a club at the end of its tail. Any predator that dared to attack it was likely to limp away in defeat with a shattered leg.

GREEN AND GROWING

By the end of the Cretaceous, flowering plants were suddenly everywhere! Their seeds were protected by a covering, so they didn't dry out and didn't get eaten so easily. Flowering plants also made new plants more quickly than other kinds. Today, most of the plants around us are flowering plants.

Tyrannosaurus rex

40 feet (12.4 m) long
T. rex preyed on large plant-eaters. Some of these vegetarians developed special protection.

Triceratops

26 feet (7.9 m)
Triceratops probably used its facial horns to defend itself from attack. But it may also have locked horns with other *Triceratops* over territory or mates.

Cretaceous Creatures

Dinosaurs could no longer travel freely from place to place after Laurasia and Gondwana broke apart. New seas acted like moats, keeping dinosaurs in certain places. As a result, new kinds of dinosaurs developed over time that were found in some places, but not in others.

Horned Ones

Ceratopsians such as *Pentaceratops*, *Torosaurus*, and *Triceratops* lived only in North America. All of the dinosaurs in this group boasted facial horns, knobby or spiky cheekbones, and neck frills.

Pentaceratops
28 feet (8.5 m) long

Torosaurus
20 feet (6 m) long

Triceratops
26 feet (7.9 m) long

Boneheads

Related dinosaurs called pachycephalosaurs lived in North America and Asia, too. These dinosaurs had very thick skulls. Because of this, they are often nicknamed "boneheads"! Some boneheads had flat heads while others had large, domed heads. Some scientists think these dinosaurs butted heads with each other the way goats do today.

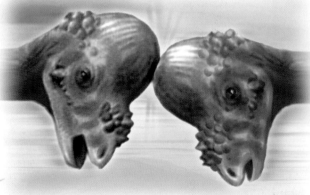
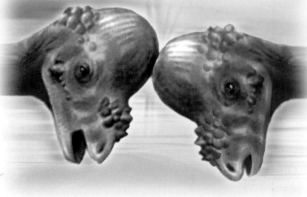

Duckbills

Hadrosaurs were plant-eating dinosaurs found mainly in North America and Asia. They lived in herds, like cattle. Hadrosaurs are also called "duckbills" because their mouths were shaped like a duck's beak. Many hadrosaurs also boasted amazing headgear. What was the headgear for? It may have helped them make loud hooting noises used to locate mates.

Parasaurolophus
6 feet (1.8 m) long

Corythosaurus
30 feet (9 m) long

Lambeosaurus
50 feet (15 m) long

Plenty of smaller meat-eaters thrived during this time, too. These creatures had big brains. Some may even have been clever enough to hunt in packs like wolves.

Utahraptor
20 feet (6 m) long
Utahraptor menaced the plant-eaters of western North America during the Early Cretaceous, long before *T. rex* even existed. Utahraptor was less than half the size of *T. rex*. Its fingers and toes bore sharp claws. Each hind foot also boasted an extra-large claw with a tip that never touched the ground and stayed razor-sharp. These meat hooks were over 12 inches (30 cm) long.

Velociraptor
6 feet (1.8 m) long

Deinonychus
10 feet (3 m) long

Super Slashers
Deinonychus and *Velociraptor* slashed prey with super-size claws, too. Only young *Deinonychus* were completely feather-covered. They lived in North America during the Early Cretaceous, after *Utahraptor*'s reign of terror was over. *Velociraptor* hunted in Asia during the Late Cretaceous.

TRIASSIC PERIOD 🦖 JURASS

DINO DIET KEY

● Meat-eater
● Plant-eater

● Herrerasaurus

● Eoraptor

● Herrerasaurus

● Coelophysis

● Plateosaurus

● Plateosaurus

● Stegosauru

● Diplodocus

● Allosaurus

● Brachiosaurus
(late Jurassic/early Cretaceous

PREHISTORIC TIME ▶ PALEOZOIC ERA

550 million years ago (mya)

Utahraptor

Velociraptor

Pinacosaurus

Parasaurolophus

Pachycephalosaurus

Tyrannosaurus rex

Stegosaurus
Fossil Bed

Triceratops

Dromaeosaurus

TRIASSIC	JURASSIC	CRETACEOUS		
	MESOZOIC ERA		CENOZOIC ERA	
248 mya	206 mya	144 mya	65 mya	today

End of the Dinosaurs

About 65 million years ago, a giant space rock called an asteroid slammed into Earth. This asteroid was 6 to 9 miles (10 to 15 km) wide. It left a crater in the Gulf of Mexico 112 miles (180 km) wide—big enough to hold the island of Hawaii.

The asteroid did much more than just leave a big hole in the ground. It may also have wiped out the dinosaurs.

When the asteroid smacked into Earth, it kicked up tons of dust and dirt that blocked the sun. Vinegarlike acid rain fell from the sky. In this poisonous, dark environment, plants died. Without plants, the plant-eating dinosaurs starved to death. Meat-eating dinosaurs then died out, too.

Is this how dinosaurs became extinct? Many scientists think so. Other scientists have different theories.

Continental drift 65 million years ago caused many volcanoes to erupt all at the same time. Gases and ash from these eruptions may have darkened the skies, cooling the world and causing plants to die. Or perhaps the dinosaurs died out slowly because the world's climate changed. Continental drift also made sea levels drop. This caused weather in some places to be colder in winter and hotter in summer—too big a change for the dinosaurs to endure.

WIPE OUT!

Dinosaurs weren't the only creatures to die in this mass extinction. Many kinds of sea creatures, lizards, and marsupials—mammals that bear young in pouches, like kangaroos—disappeared from northern continents, too. The extinction spared animals such as turtles, frogs, crocodiles, birds, and many kinds of mammals. Scientists aren't sure why.

Survivor!
Mammals like this ratlike creature (left) not only survived the mass extinction, they thrived.

Dromaeosaurus
6 feet (1.8 m) long
Dromaeosaurus was a feathered cousin of *Velociraptor*. Scientists think these dinosaurs were sisters to the bird line.

19

Dinosaur history is written in stone. All we know about dinosaurs has been carefully chipped out of rocks and dirt around the world by teams of paleontologists.

Only a few dinosaurs ever became fossils. Somehow their bodies or bones got covered by sand, mud, or water. Over a very long time, minerals seeped in and changed the bone to stone. Then, millions of years later, erosion and other forces of nature uncover the fossils.

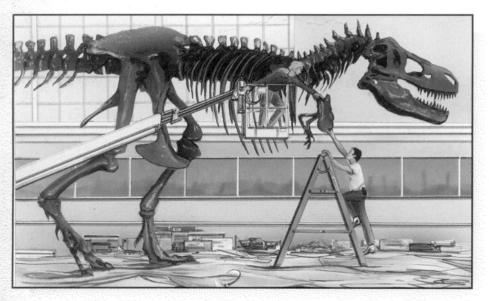

Age-old Puzzles
Scientists put fossil bones back together like the pieces of a model kit. These ancient model kits, however, are often missing many pieces. A fossil bed may contain a jumble of bones from different dinosaurs.

1. A dinosaur body washes into a river. Soon only the bones are left.

2. The skeleton is covered by sediments like sand or mud. Over time, bone turns to stone while more sediment layers build up.

3. Movements deep inside Earth bring the bones to the surface. Erosion uncovers the bones for people to find.

DRAGON BONES?

People knew about fossils long before anybody knew about dinosaurs. In ancient times, people thought they were the bones of dragons or giants. Then, in the 1790s, a French scientist named Georges Cuvier realized that some bones he had were the jaws of an extinct sea reptile. This sparked great interest in fossils. By the early 1800s, fossils were studied to figure out what kinds of ancient animals they once were. At first, scientists thought dinosaurs looked like big lizards, with sprawling legs. By the end of the 1800s, they realized that dinosaurs stood upright on their legs, like horses and birds.

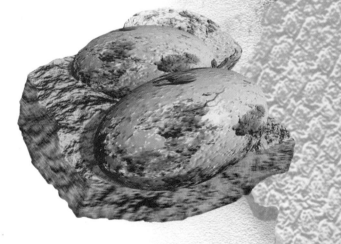

Not Just Bones
Other fossil finds include teeth and eggs. Some fossil eggs even contain fossils of baby dinosaurs. Fossil footprints give us clues about how dinosaurs walked and where they traveled. Fossil prints of skin, scales, and feathers hint at how dinosaurs looked. Fossilized droppings show what they ate.

Dinosaurs in the News

Dinosaurs are still making headlines even 65 million years after they all died out. Why?

Sometimes scientists learn new things about old fossils. Computers help scientists figure out how dinosaurs might have moved. Computerized models of *Diplodocus* suggest that it probably could not reach up high with its neck, only forward. Ideas like this make us take another look at dinosaurs we thought we knew well.

News stories also tell us about new dinosaurs. In China, paleontologists set the scientific world on its head when they dug up fossils of feathered dinosaurs! So far, they don't know just how the creatures are related to birds. The most ancient bird ever found dates back 150 million years. The feathered dinosaurs date back no more than 135 million years.

Scientists may yet prove that birds and dinosaurs evolved from the same ancestors. Meanwhile, the "fearfully great lizards" still rule—towering over us in museums and coming to life again in books and movies.

DO YOU KNOW?

Why did non-flying dinosaurs need feathers? Scientists think they helped babies stay warm. Feathers for flying evolved later.

climate The weather that exists across a large area over a long period of time.

continent A single large mass of land.

continental drift The movements of continents across the surface of Earth.

Cretaceous A period of time that began about 144 million years ago and ended 65 million years ago. Dinosaurs died out at the end of this period.

extinct Gone forever.

fossil The remains or imprint of a living thing found in ancient rocks.

Jurassic A period of time that began about 206 million years ago and ended about 144 million years ago.

mammal A group of animals that have fur and feed their babies on milk. The mammals that lived during the time of the dinosaurs were smaller than dogs. When the dinosaurs died, mammals spread out and thrived. Humans are a type of mammal.

paleontologist A scientist who studies ancient plants and animals.

predator An animal that hunts other animals for food.

prey Animals that are hunted and eaten by predators.

reptile A group of animals with scaly skin that lay shelled eggs. Crocodiles are reptiles. Dinosaurs were also reptiles.

Triassic A period of time that began about 248 million years ago and ended about 206 million years ago. The first dinosaurs appeared about halfway through this period.